Copyright © 2020 Justin Rossow and Next Step Press

ISBN: 9798605803331 · Imprint: Independently published

Cover design: Brett Jordan, bit.ly/brett_blog

Cover image: Elisa Schultz, www.elisaschulzphotography.com

Typefaces: Montserrat & Raleway

Special thanks to Ellen Davis for copy editing, to Elisa Schultz for the cover photo, and to Brett Jordan for design work.

I am grateful to Brendan Knorp for music layout and Linda Ekong for getting the illustrations into their final, digital form.

Kip Fox was a joy to work with, and this project would not have happened without the diligent direction of Lead Illustrator Valerie Matyas and the gifted artists from Visual Faith Ministry.

We want to help resource your congregation or small group. Templates of the Secret Code Prayer and the Stained Glass Prayer are found on pages 132-133 of this book for you to copy and use.

If you would like to reproduce any other pages, please email Innovation@FindMyNextStep.org to receive permission. The illustrations belong to the artists. We want you to be able to use these illustrations to help people delight in taking a next step following Jesus. In order to use them, you need express permission from Next Step Press, which we are glad to give

Let's talk.

D1560406

www.findmynextstep.org

When from Death I'm Free

A Hymn Journal for Holy Week

To access recordings of each of these songs, visit
https://www.FindMyNextStep.org/Music

A Note from the Lead Illustrator

In our fast-paced, hurried world of distraction, putting color to paper is a welcome exit ramp off the digital superhighway and onto the slower path of creative unwind.

Whether you choose to use colored pencils, markers, or paints, allow yourself time to linger with these hymns, songs, meditations, and Scripture verses. Use the act of drawing or coloring as an excuse to slow down.

We left some of the pages blank, in case your colors bleed through. You still might want to try an inexpensive, flexible cutting board under your work to protect other pages.

Gelatos, distress crayons, watercolor, or gel pens all offer varying shades of pigment and interest to your work. If drawing isn't your forte, try tracing, stencils, stamps, or stickers. There are no real rules, only launching points.

You don't have to consider yourself particularly creative to use this book. But you may be surprised what the Holy Spirit will do if you allow yourself a bit of grace and opportunity.

Blessings on the journey,

Valerie E. Matyas
Visual Faith Ministry

A Note from the Author

The great musician J. S. Bach finished his compositions with the letters "SDG," short for Soli Deo Gloria: "To God alone be the glory."

You probably knew that. But you may not have known that the maestro began his work with the letters "JJ," for Jesu, Jura: "Jesus, help!"

I shared that story with the talented Visual Faith artists on our team when we first imagined this project together. I like to think our effort has been sheltered under the umbrella of that plea of dependence ever since.

As our work on this resource draws to a close, we add our own SDG, and invite you to begin—to begin this Hymn Journal, to begin each sketch or meditation or faith experiment, to begin your next step following Jesus—we invite you to begin with that attitude of openhanded dependence.

In your prayers, in your songs, in your art, in your life, remember the simple prayer, "Jesus, help!" It's a prayer Jesus loves to answer.

JJ, and SDG,

Justin Rossow
Next Step Press

JJ

1. What Wondrous Love Is This?

Author Unknown

Text and tune:
Public domain

1. What won-drous love is this, O my soul, O my soul! What
2. When I was sink-ing down, sink-ing down, sink-ing down, When
3. To God and to the Lamb I will sing, I will sing; To
4. And when from death I'm free, I'll sing on, I'll sing on; And

won-drous love is this, O my soul!__ What won-drous love is
I was sink-ing down, sink-ing down, When I was sink-ing
God and to the Lamb I will sing.__ To God and to the
when from death I'm free, I'll sing on.__ And when from death I'm

this that caused the Lord of bliss To bear the dread-ful curse for my
down Be-neath God's righ-teous frown, Christ laid a-side His crown for my
Lamb Who is the great "I AM," While mil-lions join the theme, I will
free, I'll sing and joy-ful be, And thro' e-ter-ni-ty, I'll sing

soul, for my soul, To bear the dread-ful curse for my soul.
soul, for my soul, Christ laid a-side His crown for my soul.
sing, I will sing, While mil-lions join the theme, I will sing.
on, I'll sing on, And thro' e-ter-ni-ty, I'll sing on.

1 Corinthians 15:21-26 (ESV)

*For as by a man
came death,
by a man
has come also
the resurrection of the dead.*

*For as in Adam
all die,
so also in Christ
shall all be made alive.*

*But each in his own order:
Christ the firstfruits,
then at his coming
those who belong to Christ.*

*Then comes the end,
when he delivers the kingdom
to God the Father
after destroying every rule
and every authority and power.*

*For he must reign
until he has put all his enemies
under his feet.
The last enemy to be destroyed
is death.*

When From Death I'm Free

"The last enemy to be destroyed." That's what Paul calls Death. Not a companion. Not a door. Not a comfort or a resting place.

An enemy.

Of course, in Jesus, death has already lost its power to cause fear. Those who die in Christ are at peace in His presence. By His rest in the tomb, Jesus set aside as holy all the tombs of all His saints. So in one sense, Death is a kind of repose, a respite from the labor of living.

But in another, perhaps more central sense, Jesus isn't done with His saving acts until Death, that last enemy to be destroyed, is finally and completely done away with forever.

When you die, your soul rests with Jesus. But you were created to be a physical as well as spiritual being; your soul and your body belong together, by divine design.

So as long as any human body of someone Jesus loves lies in a grave, Jesus isn't content with the status quo. His work isn't fully finished. His victory is not yet completely complete.

Jesus loves your *body*. Jesus died for your *body*. *Your body* is going to rise.

Come quickly, Lord.

What wondrous love is this,
O my soul, O my soul,
what wondrous love is this, O my soul!
What wondrous love is this
that caused the Lord of bliss
to bear the dreadful curse
for my soul, for my soul,
to bear the dreadful curse for my soul!

When I was sinking down,
sinking down, sinking down,
when I was sinking down, sinking down;
when I was sinking down
beneath God's righteous frown,
Christ laid aside His crown
for my soul, for my soul,
Christ laid aside His crown for my soul!

To God and to the Lamb,
I will sing, I will sing,
to God and to the Lamb, I will sing;
to God and to the Lamb,
who is the great I AM,
while millions join the theme,
I will sing, I will sing,
while millions join the theme, I will sing!

And when from death I'm free,
I'll sing on, I'll sing on,
and when from death I'm free, I'll sing on;
and when from death I'm free,
I'll sing and joyful be,
and through eternity
I'll sing on, I'll sing on,
and through eternity I'll sing on!

Visual Faith Experiment

As you sing through this hymn or meditate on related Scripture, write out a verse that seems especially significant to you right now. Your creative expression doesn't have to be anything fancy. The benefit is in the time you spend praying or contemplating while also sketching, writing, coloring, or drawing. You don't have to be a professional; just engage the Word and the Spirit in a variety of ways.

And when from death I'm free

I'll sing on...

I'll sing and joyful be,

And through eternity I'll sing on!

VM 2020

2. On That Morning

Words & Music by Kip Fox

Of this one thing I am cer - tain, I am blessed be -
What a gift it is, my Sa - vior longed so deep - ly
Love be - yond all com - pre - hen - sion, God Him - self be -
I will lift His name in re - verence un - til I have

yond com - pare. Je - sus saw me lost and bro - ken
for my heart. Hea - ven could not hold His fa - vor
com - ing man. Sid - ing with the worst of - fen - ders,
reached the end. When I rise to stand be - fore Him,

and re - fused to leave me there.
un - til I re - ceived my part.
of - fer - ing His ho - ly hands.
I will sing this song a - gain.

On the earth, He shared my bur - den,

on the cross He bore my shame,

On that night death had it's way, but

on that morn - ing I was saved.

Genesis 3:12-15 (NIV)

The man said,
"The woman you
put here with me—she
gave me some fruit from the tree,
and I ate it."

Then the LORD God said
to the woman, "What is this you have done?"

The woman said,
"The serpent deceived me, and I ate."

So the LORD God said
to the serpent, "Because you have done this,

"Cursed are you above all livestock
 and all wild animals!
You will crawl on your belly
 and you will eat dust
 all the days of your life.
And I will put enmity
 between you and the woman,
 and between your offspring and hers;

he will crush your head,
 and you will strike his heel."

On That Night Death Had Its Way

A venomous snake striking your heel is just as deadly as stomping on a snake's head. The question isn't which blow is worse; the question is, what happens next?

From our perspective, after the fact, we usually view the death of Jesus on the cross as a victory for our side. And it is. But from Genesis 3 on, the death of the Seed of the Woman has also been viewed as a kind of defeat.

The cross is the enemy winning; the open tomb is God overturning defeat.

Jesus didn't deserve death. In fact, Jesus wasn't even subject to death. But the sinless Son of God submitted Himself to death's authority.

And death had its way with Him. By the time the lifeless body of Jesus is tenderly laid in a borrowed tomb, death had won, without remainder. But you know now, that's not the end of the story.

What would change in your life if you knew, down to your bones, that even total defeat is not the final answer? What if your abject failure, your persistent sin, your heartbreaking loss, didn't count as the final word?

What if you had a Savior who was completely defeated, and still won? What would you do then? Jesus took a death blow, and got right back up. For you.

Of this one thing I am certain:
I am blessed beyond compare.
Jesus saw me lost and broken
and refused to leave me there.

What a gift it is, my Savior
longed so deeply for my heart
heaven could not hold His favor
until I received my part.

On the earth He shared my burden;
on the cross He bore my shame;
on that night death had its way,
but on that morning I was saved.

Love beyond all comprehension:
God Himself becoming man,
siding with the worst offenders,
offering His holy hands.

On the earth He shared my burden;
on the cross He bore my shame;
on that night death had its way,
but on that morning I was saved.

When the stone was rolled away,
when He walked out of the grave,
all my nights returned to day.

I will lift His name in reverence
until I have reached the end.
When I rise to stand before Him
I will sing this song again:

On the earth He shared my burden;
on the cross He bore my shame;
on that night death had its way,
but on that morning I was saved.

Visual Faith Experiment

Failure and defeat are a common part of our experience in a fallen and sinful world. On the cross, Jesus entered into our defeat. In His resurrection, Jesus turned failure into victory.

Failure is a difficult burden to carry. Jesus invites you to lay that burden at the foot of His cross. You don't have to make excuses. You don't have to justify your failures. Jesus receives you as you are.

Inside the white cross on the next page, pencil in some failures that burden you. Hold those failures before Jesus.

Then color over them in dark and confident colors: Jesus is alive, and your failures are not permanent!

When the stone was rolled a - way, when He walked out of the grave, All my nights re-turned to day.

3. Ride On, Ride On in Majesty

Text: H. Milman
Tune: Unknown

Text and tune:
Public domain

Luke 19:37-38, 41-44 (ESV)

When he came near the place where the
road goes down the Mount of Olives,
the whole crowd of disciples began joyfully
to praise God in loud voices for all the
miracles they had seen:

"Blessed is the king
* who comes in the name of the Lord!"*

"Peace in heaven and glory in the highest!"

As he approached Jerusalem
and saw the city,

he wept over it

and said, "If you, even you, had only known on
this day what would bring you peace—but
now it is hidden from your eyes.

"The days will come upon you
when your enemies will
build an embankment against you
and encircle you
and hem you in on every side...

"They will not leave one stone on another,
because you did not recognize
the time of God's coming to you."

In Lowly Pomp, Ride on to Die

Surrounded by praise, the Savior King climbs the hill outside Jerusalem. The whole city lies magnificently before Him. The Temple gleams in the late afternoon sun. Shouts of joy shake the countryside. And the hero of the story ...

Weeps. He sobs. He deeply mourns the tragedy playing out in front of Him.

Each blessing, each shout of joy cuts like a knife; for although the crowd rightfully acclaims this King, they will utterly reject the Kingdom He comes to bring. Rejecting the Kingdom will ultimately lead to their destruction.

The gentle heart of Jesus is pierced. He weeps over the very same people who will soon be shouting for His crucifixion.

That tender compassion is exactly what Jesus feels for you. Jesus wants you to know peace, true peace; Jesus wants you to welcome your King; Jesus wants His Kingdom to be *yours*, now and forever.

So this humble King completes His journey. He climbs the difficult hill to the throne of the cross. He bows His meek head to be crowned with thorn. And in that sacrificial moment, the Kingdom comes. Jesus takes His power and reigns; for you.

Ride on, ride on, in majesty!
Hark! All the tribes hosanna cry.
O Savior meek, pursue Thy road,
with palms and scattered garments strowed.

Ride on, ride on, in majesty!
In lowly pomp ride on to die.
O Christ, Thy triumphs now begin
o'er captive death and conquered sin.

Ride on, ride on, in majesty!
The angel armies of the sky
look down with sad and wondering eyes
to see the approaching Sacrifice.

Ride on, ride on, in majesty!
Thy last and fiercest strife is nigh;
the Father on His sapphire throne
awaits His own anointed Son.

Ride on, ride on, in majesty!
In lowly pomp ride on to die.
Bow Thy meek head to mortal pain.
then take, O Christ, Thy power and reign.

Visual Faith Experiment

The crowds are shouting Hosanna to welcome their king; but Jesus mourns.

The Hebrew phrase from which we get the word "Hosanna" came to be used as a welcoming shout of praise and expectation; but at its root "Hosanna" means, "O, Save Us!"

How often do we see what Jesus is doing, but get it wrong? How many times have our shouts of joy brought tears to the Lord's eyes? How often have we hoped for success and forgotten how much we need saving?

Until the King comes again in glory, we, the people of the Kingdom, will always be a mixed bag. Sometimes our lives will reflect a godly joy; and sometimes what we long for makes Jesus weep.

As you add color to the art on the following page, use shades of green and shades of blue. As you use the green shades, remember the shouts of Hosanna: give Jesus praise and welcome Him again as your King.

And then, as you use shades of blue, remember the tears of Jesus. Mourn the sin and confusion and misunderstanding in the world and in your own life. Ask Him again to save you.

Greens and blues: joy, sorrow; a kingly welcome and a plea for help, all focused on Jesus.

4. The King Is Calling

Words & Music by Kip Fox

Sing for Joy the King is calling

COME

Sing for Joy

KHelmreich

Luke 14:16-23 (NIV)

Jesus replied: "A certain man was preparing a great banquet and invited many guests. At the time of the banquet he sent his servant to tell those who had been invited, 'Come, for everything is now ready.'

"But they all alike began to make excuses. The first said, 'I have just bought a field, and I must go and see it. Please excuse me.'

"Another said, 'I have just bought five yoke of oxen, and I'm on my way to try them out. Please excuse me.' Still another said, 'I just got married, so I can't come.'

"The servant came back and reported this to his master. Then the owner of the house became angry and ordered his servant, 'Go out quickly into the streets and alleys of the town and bring in the poor, the crippled, the blind and the lame.'

"'Sir,' the servant said, 'what you ordered has been done, but there is still room.'

"Then the master told his servant, 'Go out to the roads and country lanes and compel them to come in, so that my house will be full."

Hungry and Helpless

The self-sufficient guests in Jesus' parable show one way we tend to respond to God's kingdom invitation. They have already RSVP'd yes, but after the caterer has all the food in warming trays, these ingrates beg off. They are too busy. They can't be bothered.

If you are self-sufficient in your spiritual life, you will have trouble needing Jesus. The poor in spirit—they receive the Kingdom as a gift. The little children, who can do nothing for themselves, they enter in.

Outsiders. Castaways. Unwanted. Unworthy. Hungry. Helpless. Come like that to Jesus, and you will find a joyful welcome!

And watch it! False humility is as damaging as false pride. The poorest of the poor in the parable know they are not worthy, that they cannot return the invitation, that they don't own the right kind of party clothes and couldn't afford the postage for a thank-you note.

The Master says, "Compel them to come in." Because they will feel morally obligated to refuse. Jesus knows you are not worthy and that you can't repay; He wants you at His feast, anyway. His invitation is both gracious and compelling. Say yes.

Come, every beating heart
that longs to find its worth;
come, every aching soul
in need of something more.

Come with your questions,
come with your doubts—
bring them to the Lord.

Come, all you castaways,
left out of every crowd;
come, all you outsiders,
unwanted until now.

You are a people.
You have a place
waiting with the Lord.

Troubled and restless,
hungry and helpless:
sing for joy, the King is calling,
strong in justice, rich in mercy!
Sing for joy, the King is calling
and His love is never-ending.

Come, all you servants
with no candle left to burn;
Come, every broken body
tired from years of work.

Lay down your tools;
lift up your hands.
Lift them to the Lord!

Troubled and restless,
hungry and helpless:
sing for joy, the King is calling,
strong in justice, rich in mercy!
Sing for joy, the King is calling
and His love is never-ending.

Lift up a shout!
Our King is full of grace.
Lift up a shout!
He's worthy of our praise.

Troubled and restless,
hungry and helpless:
sing for joy, the King is calling,
strong in justice, rich in mercy!
Sing for joy, the King is calling
and His love is never-ending.

Full of love and grace and truth,
the King, the King is calling you!

Visual Faith Experiment

Prayerfully consider people in your life who seem troubled or restless, hungry or helpless. Choose one name to put in the center of the stained glass window, on the next page.

Begin praying for that person by name and shading in that center space as you pray. You might use a colored pencil or crayon to fill in the pane, or you could draw a design with a pen or marker, or any combination. Coloring while you pray helps keep your prayer focused.

As you pray, write down any key words or ideas that jump to mind, any specific prayer requests for that person. Add as many lines as you need to create a new pane for each prayer thought.

You might add two or three words at a time and then go back to praying. Make each new pane a different color or design. When you have a new prayer thought, add a pane. Then pray as you color it in.

As you pray, consider also the relentless invitation of Jesus. Full of love and grace and truth the King, the King is calling them. And Jesus is also calling you.

Full of love and grace and truth the King,___ the King is call-ing you.

"come for everything is ready." Luke 14:17

come in that my house may be full — Luke 14:23

5. Go to Dark Gethsemane

Text: James Montgomery
Tune: Richard Redhead

Text and tune:
Public domain

1. Go to dark Geth - sem - a - ne, All who feel the
2. Fol - low to the judg - ment hall, View the Lord of
3. Cal - v'ry's mourn - ful moun - tain climb; There, a - dor - ing
4. Ear - ly has - ten to the tomb Where they laid His

tempt - er's pow'r; Your Re - deem - er's con - flict see.
life ar - raigned; Oh, the worm - wood and the gall!
at His feet, Mark that mir - a - cle of time,
breath - less clay; All is sol - i - tude and gloom.

Watch with Him one bit - ter hour; Turn not from His
Oh, the pangs His soul sus - tained! Shun not suf - f'ring,
God's own sac - ri - fice com - plete. "It is fin - ished!"
Who has tak - en Him a - way? Christ is ris'n! He

griefs a - way; Learn from Je - sus Christ to pray.
shame, or loss; Learn from Him to bear the cross.
hear Him cry; Learn from Je - sus Christ to die.
meets our eyes. Sav - ior, teach us so to rise.

Galatians 4:6 (NIV)

God sent the Spirit of his Son into our hearts, the Spirit who calls out, "Abba, Father."

Romans 8:15 (NIV)

The Spirit you received does not make you slaves, so that you live in fear again; rather, the Spirit you received brought about your adoption to sonship. And by him we cry, "Abba, Father."

Romans 8:29 (NIV)

For those God foreknew he also predestined to be conformed to the image of his Son, that he might be the firstborn among many brothers and sisters.

Mark 14:35-36 (NIV)

Going a little farther,
he fell to the ground
and prayed that if possible
the hour might pass from him.

"Abba, Father," he said,
"everything is possible for you.
"Take this cup from me.
"Yet not what I will,
but what you will."

Learn of Jesus Christ to Pray
The Spirit shapes you to be like Jesus.

Over time, the Spirit shapes the life of Jesus in you, so that you are conformed more and more to the image of the Son; that is, so that you look more like Jesus in your everyday life.

By looking at what Jesus does *for us* we catch a glimpse of what the Spirit is doing *in us*.

For us, the obedient Son prays to the Father in the Garden, prays for God's Kingdom to come and God's will to be done on earth as in heaven. In us, the Spirit shapes the prayer, "Our Father, thy Kingdom come; thy will be done..."

For us, the suffering Son picks up His cross and carries the shame and sorrow of the world. In us, the Spirit shapes a willingness to bear one another's burdens, and so fulfill the law if Christ.

For us, the sacrificial Son shows the full measure of His grace, embracing even death for those He loves. In us, the Spirit shapes a daily dying to self and pride and the need to be right.

For us, the victorious Son rises in glory. In us, the Spirit shapes resurrection life, already now, and will one day conform our lowly bodies to be like the glorious, human, risen and glorified body of Jesus. The Spirit shapes you to be like Jesus.

Be Conformed TO HIS IMAGE

Go to dark Gethsemane,
you who feel the tempter's pow'r;
your Redeemer's conflict see;
watch with Him one bitter hour;
turn not from His griefs away;
learn of Jesus Christ to pray.

Follow to the judgment hall;
view the Lord of life arraigned;
O the worm-wood and the gall!
O the pangs His soul sustained!
Shun not suff'ring, shame, or loss;
learn of Him to bear the cross.

Calv'ry's mournful mountain climb
there adoring at His feet.
Mark the miracle of time,
God's own sacrifice complete:
"It is finished!" Hear Him cry;
learn of Jesus Christ to die.

Early hasten to the tomb
where they laid His breathless clay;
all is solitude and gloom;
who hath taken Him away?
Christ is ris'n! He meets our eyes:
Savior, teach us so to rise.

Visual Faith Experiment

Choose a phrase from the Scripture verses or hymn in this chapter, one that was meaningful to you. Focus your prayer and meditation around that text by writing it out on the next page.

You can write it many times, or one time. You can color it in or leave it black and white. You can write it in any language or any style you want. But spend some time with the words.

Slow your prayers down. Invite the Spirit to be present. And talk to Jesus about being shaped to act and think and feel and pray a little more like Him this week.

6. Thieves on a Cross

Words & Music by Kip Fox

Luke 23:32-34, 39-43 (NIV)

Two other men,
both criminals,
were also led out with him
to be executed.

When they came to the place
called the Skull, they crucified him there,
along with the criminals—one on his right,
the other on his left.

Jesus said, "Father, forgive them,
for they do not know what they are doing."

One of the criminals who hung there
hurled insults at him: "Aren't you the Messiah?
Save yourself and us!"

But the other criminal rebuked him.
"Don't you fear God," he said, "since you are
under the same sentence? We are punished
justly, for we are getting what our deeds
deserve. But this man has done nothing
wrong."

Then he said, "Jesus, remember me
when you come into your kingdom."

Jesus answered him, "Truly I tell you, today
you will be with me in paradise."

Look to the Man by Our Side

Through the taunts and jeers comes a lone voice, the voice of a criminal who knows he stands under judgment, who recognizes death as the just punishment for his sins. Oh, he started out mocking Jesus; but he's been watching how this King dies.

So he doesn't say, with his fellow bandit, "Prove to me that you're a King and do things just the way I want!" Instead, he looks beyond the cross and crown of thorns, the bruises and the blood. He looks under the placard that advertises "the King of the Jews" and makes a daring prayer, a prayer of hope: "Jesus, remember me, when you come into your kingdom."

All the mockery, all the insults, all the jeers almost got it right. This Jesus is the King. By this cross the King comes into His Kingdom. And I have to imagine that the thief's eyes opened wide in amazement when he heard the reply.

"Today." Today! The Kingdom is here and now.

"Today you will be with me..."

Before this day is over, the fall from Eden will be undone, the curse will be removed, death will be defeated—

"Today you will be with me in Paradise."

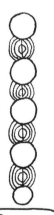

We are all thieves on a cross
meriting mutiny's cost,
destined to suffer eternal loss:
we are all thieves on a cross.

Look to the Man by our side,
guiltless and hanging to die,
praying for sinners who took His life:
look to the Man by our side.

Glory be to our Savior!
Glory be to the Lamb!
Glory be to the One
who took death in His hands!

See, how He loved us to death!
Weep now, and beat on your breast!
Watch as He summons His final breath;
see how He loved us to death!

Witness the stone rolled away.
Listen and be not afraid.
Go, and proclaim Christ is ris'n today:
Jesus has conquered the grave!

Glory be to our Savior!
Glory be to the Lamb!
Glory be to the One
who took death in His hands!

Visual Faith Experiment

One of the most remarkable promises in all the Gospels is spoken to this unremarkable thief who knows and admits he probably had this death sentence coming.

Jesus speaks that remarkable promise to you, too. The first step is not to be good, or holy, or try a little harder, or do a little better. The first step is to be like that unremarkable thief on the cross: admit your life and heart are far from God.

The grid on the next page is designed to slow your thinking and praying down, but it has one really helpful side effect: if anyone happens to glance over your shoulder, they won't be able to read your words quickly or easily. (That's why it's called The Secret Code prayer, even though it's not actually in code...)

Take this somewhat covert opportunity to confess your sins, one letter at a time, with no space between the words. Use all capital letters or all lowercase. Be as honest as you want, as honest as a thief on the cross.

When you are finished, reread the verses from Luke 23 and the text of *Thieves on a Cross*. Then write, "Father, forgive!" in colorful letters above your prayer. Use a dark colored marker, paint, or whiteout to blot out your confession. Your sins are covered by the blood of Jesus.

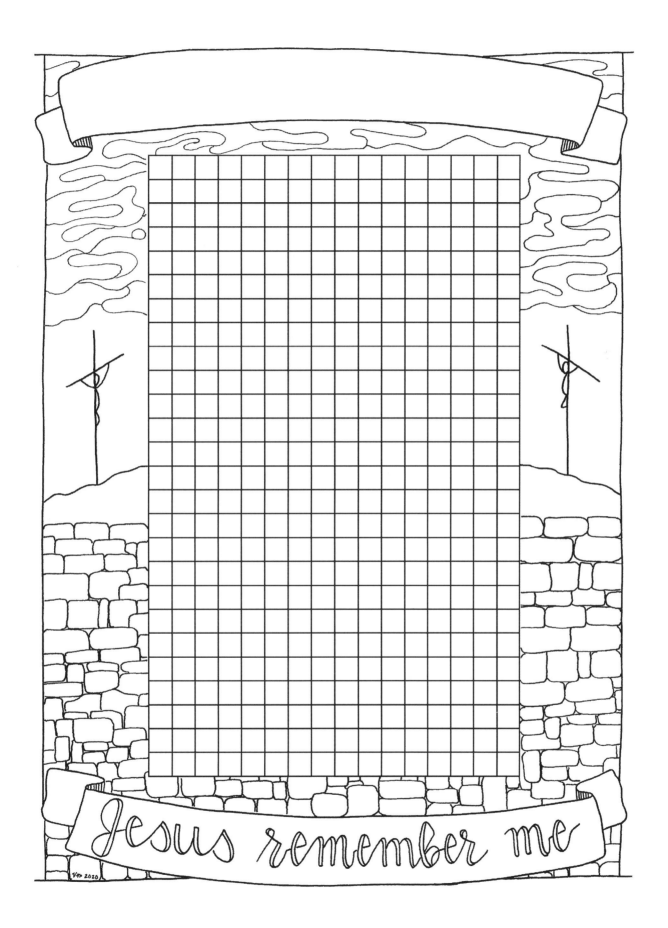

Jesus remember me

7. When I Survey the Wondrous Cross

Text: Isaac Watts
Tune: Lowell Mason

SORROW, SO AND LOVE AMAZING SO DIVINE DEMANDS MY SOUL MY LIFE MY ALL

pm 2020

Philippians 3:7-10

But whatever gain I had,
I counted as loss for the sake of Christ.
Indeed, I count everything as loss
because of the surpassing worth
of knowing Christ Jesus my Lord.

For his sake I have suffered
the loss of all things
and count them as rubbish,
in order that I may gain Christ
and be found in him,
not having a righteousness of my own
that comes from the law,
but that which comes through faith in Christ,
the righteousness from God
that depends on faith—that I may know him
and the power of his resurrection,
and may share his sufferings,
becoming like him in his death,
that by any means possible
I may attain the resurrection from the dead.

Not that I have already obtained this
or am already perfect, but I press on
to make it my own, because Christ Jesus
has made me his own.

Sorrow and Love

The teachings of Jesus are full of paradoxes. "The first will be last." "Whoever want to be greatest, must be a slave." "Those who lose their lives with save them." "Blessed are the poor in spirit, for theirs is the kingdom."

The death of Jesus is full of paradoxes. At the cross we see the greatest justice and the greatest travesty of justice combine. The symbol of kingship is interwoven with the sign of sin's curse. Sorrow is mingled with love. We boast and glory in this shame. Our greatest loss is also our greatest gain.

The lives of those who follow Jesus are full of paradoxes. You are called to love your enemies. You are spurred to constant and active engagement in a life of faith you can only passively receive. You are invited to die, but only so that you can truly live.

The cross shows us clearly the breathtaking beauty of the ugliest moment in human history. And the cross sends us out as people of paradox: people who pour themselves out, yet are never empty. People who suffer great loss, and yet own the world. People who are riddled with weakness and sin, and yet shine like the stars in their splendor.

The power of the cross turns people inside out and the world upside down. And we will never be the same.

When I survey the wondrous cross
on which the Prince of Glory died,
my richest gain I count but loss,
and pour contempt on all my pride.

Forbid it, Lord, that I should boast
save in the death of Christ, my God.
All the vain things that charm me most,
I sacrifice them to His blood.

See, from His head, His hands, His feet,
sorrow and love flow mingled down.
Did e'er such love and sorrow meet
or thorns compose so rich a crown?

Were the whole realm of nature mine,
that were a tribute far too small;
love so amazing, so divine,
demands my soul, my life, my all.

*Directions for the Visual Faith Experiment
on pages 74-75 are found on page 76.

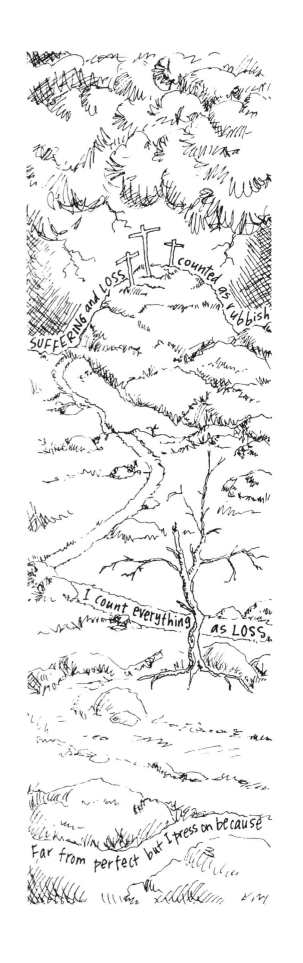

Visual Faith Experiment

Paul says he experiences in his life right now both death and resurrection, loss and new life. The apostle is quick to point out that he hasn't actually achieved perfect resurrection life ahead of The Resurrection. And he also wants his readers to grab ahold of that resurrection life already now, ahead of time.

Of course, any kind of resurrection requires a kind of death first.

Paul has his list of losses. And he also has a companion list of places where Jesus has brought strength and life in the midst of suffering and loss.

Prayerfully consider what things Jesus has removed from your life, or maybe is working to remove (things like pride or self-dependence). Write or draw your list in the margin on page 74.

Then, on page 75, add ways you have seen the Spirit work resurrection in your life, ahead of time. Where have you seen peace come out of the tomb of your pride, or joy blossom where you buried your need to be right? How has the death of your self-sufficiency brought a new life of needing Jesus?

You aren't perfect yet, but Jesus has already grabbed hold of you! Already now your list of loss and death is being transformed into a kaleidoscope of new life, ahead of schedule.

8. The Dignity of the Cross

Words & Music by Kip Fox
and Jonathan Lee

Our great - est gifts,   we bring in vain.
The weight of sin,   the guilt and shame,

Our sac - ri - fice is not e - nough.
U - pon the shoul - ders of a King.

There is a debt   Your love has paid.
You took the nails,   en - dured the pain,

You left Your throne from a - bove.___ You gave Your-self
You did not keep a - ny - thing.___

whol-ly for us___   We give our praise

whol-ly to You,___ Je - sus   No great-er price.

No great-er cost.   How high the dig - ni - ty of the cross.___

How___ deep Your love, how   wide Your arms, how

great the won - ders of what You've done. How___ deep Your love, how

wide Your arms, how   great the won - ders of what You've done.

77

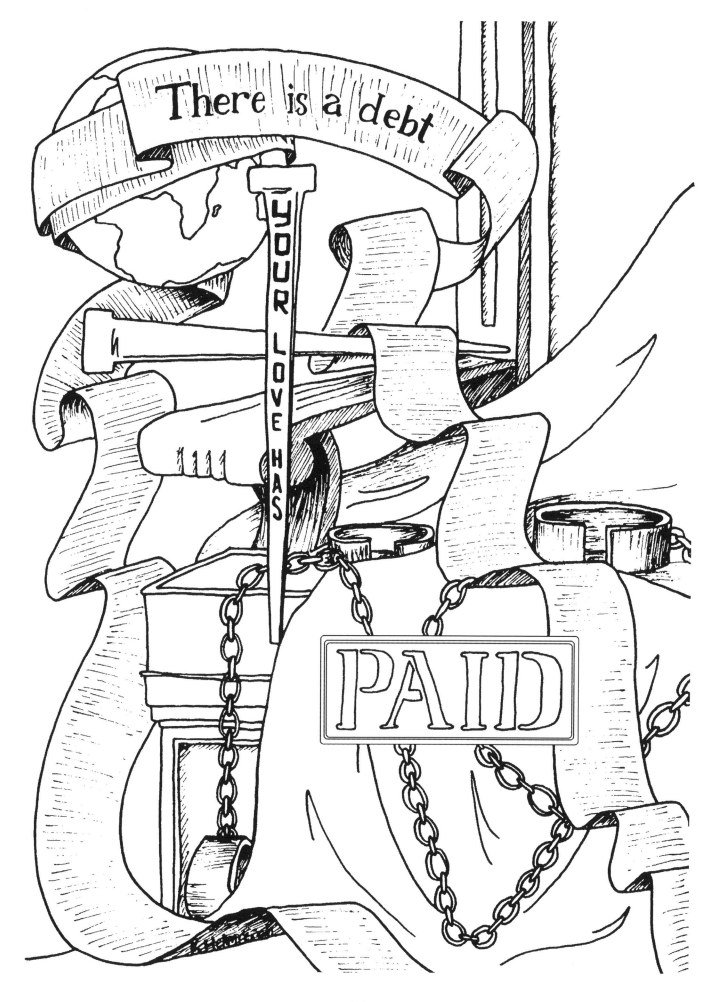

Matthew 13:44-45 (NIV)

The kingdom of heaven
is like treasure hidden in a field.
When a man found it, he hid it again,
and then in his joy
went and sold all he had
and bought that field.

Again, the kingdom of heaven
is like a merchant
looking for fine pearls.
When he found one of great value,
he went away and
sold everything he had
and bought it.

Hebrews 12:1-2 (ESV)

Let us run with endurance
the race that is set before us,
looking to Jesus,
the founder and
perfecter of our faith, who

for the joy
that was set before him

endured the cross,
despising the shame,
and is seated at the right hand
of the throne of God.

Wholly, for Us

Look again at the treasure in the field and the pearl of great price. In both cases, the one who discovers the item of value is willing to sell *absolutely everything!* That's how much the treasure and the pearl are worth.

Jesus even goes out of His way to mention the joy that comes from selling everything you have if you know it will buy you something of even greater value. "Everything I own? For that one pearl, for that one treasure? Gladly! With joy!!"

If you ever have cause to question your own value, if you ever feel like you have no worth, if your sin or failure or shame ever makes your life seem like a total waste, check your price tag.

Because your price tag reads: "The Very Life of the Son of God." Jesus read that price tag, and considered eternity with you or without you. Then *with tears of joy* Jesus sold everything He had so He could afford to buy *you*.

You were the joy set before Jesus that led Him to endure the cross, and even scorn its shame. "The cross? For that one pearl, for that one treasure? Gladly! With joy!!"

No greater price; no greater cost.

For you. You were worth it.

Our greatest gifts
we bring in vain;
our sacrifice is not enough.

There is a debt
Your love has paid;
You left your throne from above.

You gave yourself wholly for us.
We give our praise wholly to you, Jesus.
No greater price; no greater cost.
How high the dignity of the cross!

The weight of sin,
the guilt and shame,
upon the shoulders of a king.

You took the nails,
endured the pain.
You did not keep anything.

You gave yourself wholly for us.
We give our praise wholly to you, Jesus.
No greater price; no greater cost.
How high the dignity of the cross!

How deep your love!
How wide your arms!
How great the wonders
of what you've done!

Visual Faith Experiment

When we did the Stained Glass Prayer for "The King is Calling," you put the name of the person you prayed for in the center. Today, put *your own name* there. (I know; weird, right?)

Now begin shading in the central shape that holds your name; you could use a favorite color or create a pattern or meaningful design.

As you work, talk to Jesus about how He sees you. Remember, He gave Himself wholly for you, because of the joy He has in you.

As you pray, write down the key words or ideas that jump to mind, adding lines as needed to create a new pane for each. You might add two or three words at a time and then begin adding color to those panes as you pray for each one.

It's OK if you find some darker colors of confession in your window; just remember, this stained glass wants to reflect how Jesus sees you. Yes, He knows your sin; and He also thought you were a treasure, a pearl of such great value that He gave Himself wholly for you.

Ask Jesus what He likes best about you. Ask Jesus what makes Him proud of you. Invite the Spirit to give you a glimpse into the heart of the Father for you. Write that down as you pray and marvel at the love that is yours in Christ!

Who for the JOY that was set before HIM endured the CROSS

despising the shame, and is seated at the right hand of the THRONE of GOD.

-HEBREWS 12:2-

9. Stricken, Smitten, and Afflicted

Text: Thomas Kelly
Tune: Unknown

Text and tune:
Public domain

1. Strick-en, smit-ten, and af-flict-ed, See Him dy-ing on the
2. Tell me, ye who hear Him groan-ing, Was there ev-er grief like
3. Ye who think of sin but light-ly Nor sup-pose the e-vil
4. Here we have a firm foun-da-tion; Here the ref-uge of the

tree! 'Tis the Christ, by man re-ject-ed; Yes, my
His? Friends through fear His cause dis-own-ing, Foes in-
great Here may view its na-ture right-ly, Here its
lost; Christ, the rock of our sal-va-tion, His the

soul, 'tis He, 'tis He! 'Tis the long-ex-pect-ed
sult-ing His dis-tress; Man-y hands were raised to
guilt may es-ti-mate. Mark the sac-ri-fice ap-
name of which we boast. Lamb of God, for sin-ners

Proph-et, Da-vid's Son, yet Da-vid's Lord; Proofs I
wound Him, None would in-ter-vene to save; But the
point-ed, See who bears the aw-ful load; 'Tis the
wound-ed, Sac-ri-fice to can-cel guilt! None shall

see suf-fi-cient of it: 'Tis the true and faith-ful Word.
deep-est stroke that pierced Him Was the stroke that jus-tice gave.
Word, the Lord's a-noin-ted, Son of Man and Son of God.
ev-er be con-found-ed Who on Him their hope have built.

2 Corinthians 5:16-21 (NIV)

So from now on we regard no one from a worldly point of view. Though we once regarded Christ in this way, we do so no longer. Therefore,

> *if anyone is in Christ,*
> *the new creation has come:*
> *The old has gone,*
> *the new is here!*

All this is from God, who reconciled us to himself through Christ and gave us the ministry of reconciliation: that God was reconciling the world to himself in Christ, not counting people's sins against them.

And he has committed to us the message of reconciliation. We are therefore Christ's ambassadors, as though God were making his appeal through us.

> *We implore you on Christ's behalf:*
> *Be reconciled to God.*

> *God made him*
> *who had no sin*
> *to be sin for us,*
> *so that in him*
> *we might become*
> *the righteousness of God.*

Ye Who Think of Sin but Lightly

The loving face of Jesus, which shone like the sun at the Transfiguration, is now swollen and bloody; disfigured, discolored, distorted in pain.

It's just not fair. Jesus did nothing to deserve this. Jesus was life and light shining in the darkness. And the darkness pushed back. Hard.

Yet in this travesty of justice, a deeper justice is done. Jesus suffers the just consequences of sin. The ugliness and brutality of the cross *is* the ugliness and brutality of rebellion against God, *my* rebellion against God.

This is what sin looks like. This is what sin feels like. This is what sin does. This is what sin deserves.

This is what Jesus takes from me; Jesus became my sin in my place. That's *my* sin up there, on the cross. That's *my* violence and hatred and shame. Jesus takes away the worst of who I am.

In return, Jesus gives me the best of who he is. Jesus exchanges His holiness for my sin, His beauty for my distortion, His obedience for my rebellion, His life for my death.

Jesus takes my darkness to the cross. In return, I now shine like the Son.

SIN
VIOLENCE
HATRED
SHAME

BEAUTY
HOLINESS
LIFE
OBEDIENCE

Stricken, smitten, and afflicted,
see Him dying on the tree!
'Tis the Christ by man rejected;
yes, my soul, 'tis he, 'tis he!
'Tis the long-expected Prophet,
David's Son, yet David's Lord!
Proofs I see sufficient of it:
'tis the true and faithful Word.

Tell me, ye who hear Him groaning,
was there ever grief like His?
Friends thro' fear His cause disowning,
foes insulting His distress;
many hands were raised to wound Him,
none would interpose to save;
but the deepest stroke that pierced Him
was the stroke that Justice gave.

Ye who think of sin but lightly
nor suppose the evil great
here may view its nature rightly,
here its guilt may estimate.
Mark the sacrifice appointed,
see who bears the awful load;
'tis the Word, the Lord's Anointed,
Son of Man and Son of God.

Here we have a firm foundation,
here the refuge of the lost;
Christ's the Rock of our salvation,
his the name of which we boast.
Lamb of God, for sinners wounded,
sacrifice to cancel guilt!
None shall ever be confounded
who on Him their hope have built.

STRICKEN, SMITTEN, AND AFFLICTED
SEE HIM DYING ON THE TREE!
'TIS THE CHRIST BY MAN REJECTED;
YES, MY SOUL, 'TIS HE, 'TIS HE!
'TIS THE LONG-EXPECTED PROPHET,
DAVID'S SON, YET DAVID'S LORD!
PROOFS I SEE SUFFICIENT OF IT:
'TIS THE TRUE AND FAITHFUL WORD.

Visual Faith Experiment

Use words or images from the hymn or Scripture reading to explore the theme of the Great Exchange: God made Him who knew no sin to be sin for us, that in Him we might become the righteousness of God.

10. This Dust

Words & Music by Kip Fox

Lord have mer - cy on me I am
Oh what sense - less love That

rid - dled with the world's di - sease Of
You would come to join with us And

tak - ing what I want And
drink this curs - ed cup Re -

turn - ing it in - to a need
deem - ing all that we've un - done

I am flesh and blood Ne - ver good e - nough
We are flesh and blood Ne - ver good e - nough

You poured out Your love To co - ver o'er this dust

Mer - cy rains On all our shame And

wash - es all The stain a - way

Death is all a - round us, we are not af - raid.

Writ - ten is the sto - ry, emp - ty is the grave.

97

written is the story
empty is the grave

But IN FACT Christ has been RAISED from the dead the FIRST FRUITS of those who have fallen asleep. 1 COR 15:20

KAH 2020

1 Corinthians 15:1-4, 14, 17-20 (NIV)

Now, brothers and sisters,
I want to remind you of the gospel
I preached to you,
which you received
and on which
you have taken your stand.

For what I received
I passed on to you
as of first importance:

that Christ died for our sins
according to the Scriptures,
that he was buried,
that he was raised on the third day
according to the Scriptures...

If Christ has not been raised,
our preaching is useless and so is your faith...

And if Christ has not been raised,
your faith is futile; you are still in your sins.

Then those also who have
fallen asleep in Christ are lost.

If only for this life we have hope in Christ,
we are of all people most to be pitied.

But Christ has indeed
been raised from the dead,
the firstfruits of those who have fallen asleep.

Death Is All Around Us

In a culture where the dying are hermetically sealed off from the rest of our experience, I find death easy to forget, at times. And then there are times when death feels relentless, and the reminders of my own mortality refuse to be ignored.

I have watched my kids grow up with death. In a very short time, my children went from never having been to a funeral to grieving the death of two great-grandparents, a grandpa, a youth worker, and a high school friend. For starters.

My children have learned, death all around us.

And we are not afraid. So much loss in a short time meant that more than one of our kids had some separation anxiety. Every time we part, one of my teenagers still tells me that *she* loves me, and that *Jesus* loves me (even if she's just going to bed). Because, in her words, "You never know which time will be the last."

It breaks my heart that her experience has led her to think like that. And it gives me such joy and peace to know the last thing she wants to say to me, whenever that last time comes, is this: "I love you, Daddy; and Jesus loves you."

Death is all around us; we are not afraid. Written is the story, empty is the grave.

Lord have mercy on me:
I am riddled with the world's disease
of taking what I want
and turning it into a need.

I am flesh and blood,
never good enough;
you poured out your love
to cover o'er this dust.

Oh what senseless love
that you would come to join with us
and drink this cursed cup
redeeming all that we've undone.

We are flesh and blood,
never good enough;
you poured out your love
to cover o'er this dust.

And mercy reigns
on all our shame
and washes all
the stain away.

Death is all around us;
we are not afraid:
written is the story,
empty is the grave.

Death is all around us;
we are not afraid:
written is the story,
empty is the grave.

Death is all around us;
And mercy reigns
we are not afraid:
on all our shame
written is the story,
and washes all
empty is the grave.
the stain away.

Death is all around us;
we are not afraid:
written is the story,
empty is the grave.

Visual Faith Experiment

If repetition is the mother of learning, she is at least a first cousin of faith. On the next page, write out the last phrase of this song several times, in several styles, colors, or sizes. Keep repeating it over and over, just to let that truth soak in. *Death is all around us; we are not afraid: written is the story, empty is the grave.*

KAH 2020

11. I Know that My Redeemer Lives

Text: Samuel Medley
Tune: John Hatton

Text and tune:
Public domain

1. I know that my Re - deem - er lives!
2. He lives tri - um - phant from the grave;
3. He lives to bless me with His love;
4. He lives to grant me rich sup - ply;

What com - fort this sweet sen - tence gives!
He lives e - ter - nal - ly to save;
He lives to plead for me a - bove;
He lives to guide me with His eye;

He lives, He lives, who once was dead;
He lives all - glo - rious in the sky;
He lives my hun - gry soul to feed;
He lives to com - fort me when faint;

He lives, my ev - er - liv - ing head!
He lives ex - alt - ed there on high.
He lives to help in time of need.
He lives to hear my soul's com - plaint.

5. He lives to silence all my fears;
He lives to wipe away my tears;
He lives to calm my troubled heart;
He lives all blessings to impart.

6. He lives, my kind, wise, heav'nly friend,
He lives and loves me to the end;
He lives, and while He lives, I'll sing;
He lives, my Prophet, Priest, and King.

7. He lives and grants me daily breath;
He lives, and I shall conquer death;
He lives my mansion to prepare;
He lives to bring me safely there.

8. He lives, all glory to His name!
He lives, my Jesus, still the same;
Oh, the sweet joy this sentence gives:
I know that my Redeemer lives!

Job 19:23-27 (NIV)

Oh, that my words
were recorded,
that they were written
on a scroll,
that they were inscribed
with an iron tool on lead,
or engraved
in rock forever!

I know that
my redeemer lives,
and that in the end
he will stand on the earth.

And after my skin
has been destroyed,
yet in my flesh
I will see God;

I myself will see him
with my own eyes—
I, and not another.

How my heart yearns within me!

He Lives, and I Shall Conquer Death

Filled with fear and joy, the women are on their way back from the open tomb when the risen Jesus meets them on the road. Matthew goes out of his way to tell us that the women grabbed Jesus *by the feet* (Matthew 28:9).

What a strange detail! Until you understand what was common knowledge in that culture: *ghosts don't have feet.*

Mary and the other Mary are holding tightly to the physical evidence that this is Jesus, the real Jesus; the risen, human Jesus, with a real body that was dead, but is now alive. No ghost.

I think Matthew wants you to fall at the risen Lord's feet in worship. And then grab onto those physical, human, resurrection feet of Jesus.

That's a real body you have in your hands, not some spirit or memory or disembodied soul. Those feet are a tangible promise for the future of your human body: a real, human, physical, resurrection existence. You won't be an angel. You won't be a disembodied soul. You won't be a ghost. Your body will rise from the dead.

Your Redeemer lives! And in the end, He will stand upon the earth. And *in your flesh*, you will see God. So grab the resurrected feet of Jesus, and hang on for dear life!

Alleluia

Alleluia

I know that my Redeemer lives;
what comfort this sweet sentence gives!
He lives, He lives, who once was dead;
He lives, my ever-living Head.

He lives triumphant from the grave,
He lives eternally to save,
He lives all-glorious in the sky,
He lives exalted there on high.

He lives to bless me with His love,
He lives to plead for me above,
He lives my hungry soul to feed,
He lives to help in time of need.

He lives to grant me rich supply,
He lives to guide me with His eye,
He lives to comfort me when faint,
He lives to hear my soul's complaint.

He lives to silence all my fears,
He lives to wipe away my tears,
He lives to calm my troubled heart,
He lives all blessings to impart.

He lives, my kind, wise, heav'nly friend,
He lives and loves me to the end;
He lives, and while He lives, I'll sing;
He lives, my Prophet, Priest, and King.

He lives and grants me daily breath;
He lives and I shall conquer death;
He lives my mansion to prepare;
He lives to bring me safely there.

He lives, all glory to His name!
He lives, my Jesus, still the same.
Oh, the sweet joy this sentence gives,
"I know that my Redeemer lives!"

Visual Faith Experiment

Use the "Secret Code Prayer" on the next page to slow down and focus your praise. Begin with "CHRISTISRISENALLELUIA." Don't leave space between the words and don't use punctuation. Choose either all capital or all lowercase letters. Then pray, one letter at a time.

This Secret Code Prayer often works best if you give yourself a time limit. Five minutes is pretty good. The goal is not to fill up the whole grid, but merely to spend a focused time in prayer. When your timer goes off, finish your thought and end with "HEISRISENINDEEDALLELUIA."

12. We Will Rise

Words & Music by Kip Fox
and Brady Toops

For a sin - ful world You had come to die. For the
For the help - less ones, for the weak and poor, for the

love You'd shown, You were cru - ci - fied They put
hurt - ing soul, there is hope in store. For the

on Your crown, and the blood came down, so that
stone that day, it was rolled a - way,

we could have new life.___ We will

rise up from these ash - es like You rose up from the

grave. Through the trou - bles of these a - ges and the
And we'll stand with You in glo - ry on that

tri - als of our days. We will
re - sur - rec - tion day.

rise up! We will rise up! We will

rise up! We will rise up!

1 Corinthians 15:36-37, 42-43, 54-57 (ESV)

What you sow
does not come to life
unless it dies.

And what you sow
is not the body that is to be,
but a bare kernel...

So is it with the resurrection of the dead.

What is sown is perishable;
what is raised is imperishable.

It is sown in dishonor;
it is raised in glory.

It is sown in weakness;
it is raised in power...

When the perishable
puts on the imperishable,
and the mortal
puts on immortality,
then shall come to pass
the saying that is written:

"Death is swallowed up in victory.
"O death, where is your victory?
"O death, where is your sting?"

The sting of death is sin,
and the power of sin is the law.
But thanks be to God,
who gives us the victory
through our Lord Jesus Christ.

On That Resurrection Day

The Easter lily has long been an image for life that comes after death, and with good reason! Just think of the difference between the lily bulb and flower: the bulb is small, hard, ugly, and smells like death. The flower, on the other hand, is large, beautiful, vibrant, smells like life.

If you hadn't experienced it, it might be kind of hard to believe that a hard, dead bulb can be buried in the ground and, after a time, be transformed into a vibrant, beautiful flower.

And you and I have planted enough loved ones in the ground to know that it can be kind of hard to believe that this stiff and lifeless corpse will someday be full of life again.

The body of Jesus didn't go into the ground as a *bulb* and then come out of the ground a *bulb*. His resurrection was not like that of Lazarus. No, Jesus went into the ground as a bulb, and Jesus came out again as a *grown plant in full bloom*.

In the same way, your body will one day be buried in a fallen and sinful world and raised in the New Creation. Your body will be planted a bulb; your body will be raised a full-grown flower. That Resurrection Day will not be a day of digging bulbs out of the ground before the winter frost; it will be a day of glorious blossoms!

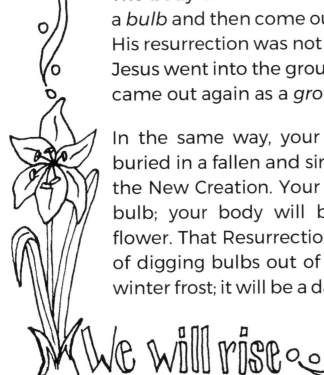

We will rise

For a sinful world
you had come to die.
For the love you'd shown
you were crucified.
They put on your crown,
and the blood came down,
so that we could have new life.

We will rise up from the ashes
like you rose up from the grave
through the troubles of these ages
and the trials of our days.

For the helpless ones,
for the weak and poor,
for the hurting soul
there is hope in store.
For the stone that day,
it was rolled away
so that we could have new life.

We will rise up from the ashes
like you rose up from the grave
through the troubles of these ages
and the trials of our days.

We will rise up from the ashes
like you rose up from the grave,
and we'll stand with you in glory
on that Resurrection Day.

We will rise up!

Visual Faith Experiment

The Apostle Paul makes the point that different seeds produce different kinds of plants. While your New Creation body will be almost unbelievably different from your current body, it will somehow be the same you, just full-grown, and uniquely different from everybody else and their unique, full-grown, physical, human, New Creation bodies.

On the next page, think of some people who are important to you and about what makes them unique. In words, or shapes, or colors, create a bouquet of people you love.

What's Your Next Step?

We hope this Hymn Journal has been a useful tool as you seek to get to know Jesus better. Being intentional about your faith isn't easy: keep it up!

As you try to take a next step following Jesus, we have found that having a regular time with a regular person or two is a real help. Get together a couple times a month, invite the Spirit to be present, and simply talk about these three questions:

- What's Jesus speaking into your life?
- What response is Jesus shaping in you?
- What promise from Jesus is guiding your next step?

If you don't know how to begin to answer one of those questions, that's an invitation from Jesus to turn to Him again in need.

Your next step might be, "Talk to someone about figuring out my next step." Maybe your prayer is, "Jesus, I have no idea what I am supposed to be doing right now."

Needing Jesus is the single most important trait of any disciple. He won't give up on you.

For the Record

Look back over the work you have done in this Hymn Journal. Where have you grown? What have you learned? What was meaningful to you? What was interesting or confusing or helpful or frustrating? What emotions did you experience as you walked through this book?

If you find a common theme, you could wonder with Jesus what He is up to in our life. But whether you have a clear direction for a next step or only a vague inkling, try to put something down in each of the following areas.

If you get stuck, phone a friend. If you just don't know, let that open question be your next step. Jesus is with you, no matter what.

Because I like being intentional in my faith walk, I'm looking for what Jesus is inviting me into next. After prayerful conversation, here is

My Next Step:

Because I know we follow Jesus better when we follow Him together, I'm going to invite a couple of people to walk with me for a ways on this faith journey. So I'll take this next step

With These People:

Because I know I am not up for this journey on my own, and because I want to learn more and more how to depend on Jesus in my everyday life, I am consciously holding on to

This Promise From Jesus That Guides My Next Step:

Something to Share

We follow Jesus better when we follow Him together. That means we all have something to learn, and something to share.

Find one thing that made a difference in your faith or life as you have experienced this Hymn Journal. Now share that experience with a friend.

Maybe it was a visual faith experiment or a particular hymn verse. Maybe it was a specific thought or Scripture reading. Maybe the time you set aside in God's presence helped you see something you had forgotten or had never seen before.

Take one thing—any one thought, or drawing, or reading, or hymn—that had an impact on you, and share it with someone else. Try to express why it was meaningful for you. Invite them to run an experiment and see if it might be meaningful for them, too.

By sharing even one thing with someone else, you plant that Word deeper in your own heart and life. You also extend an invitation for someone else to begin to wonder what Jesus is up to in their life.

Following Jesus can be scary and exciting and difficult and rewarding; and it's just more fun when you share the experience with others.

We follow Jesus better when we follow Him together. Thanks for sharing this leg of the journey with us; may Jesus guide and bless your next step on this adventure of faith!

What I shared:

Who I shared it with:

How it went:

The Secret Code Prayer

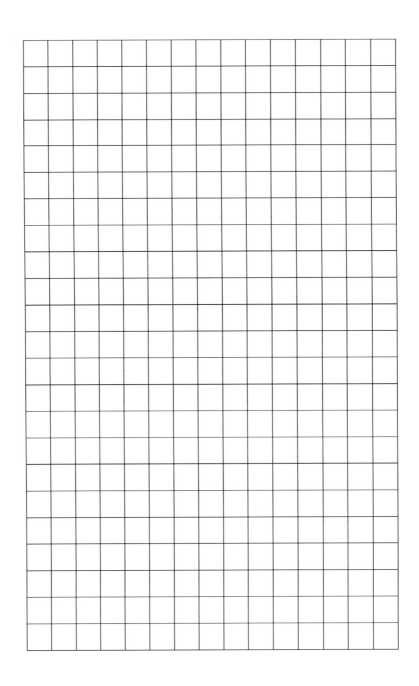

The Stained Glass Prayer

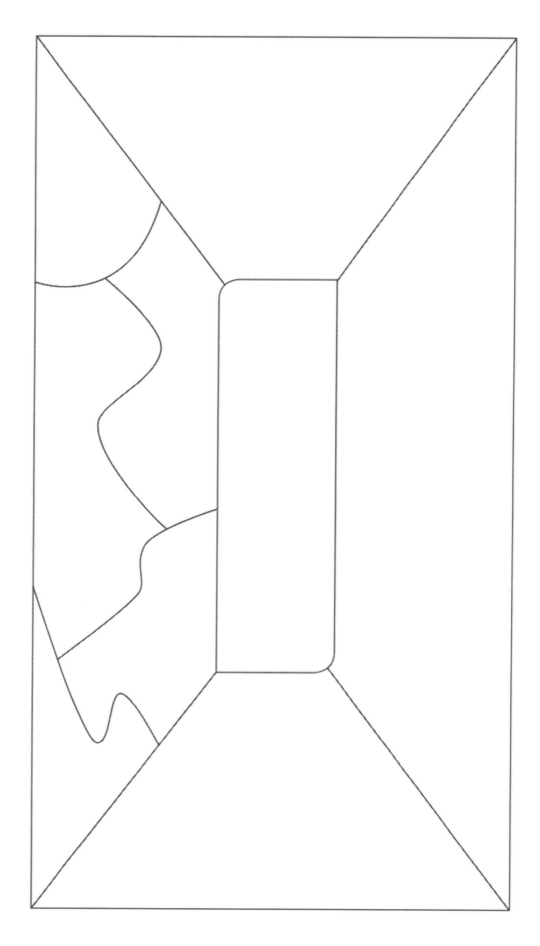

About Visual Faith Ministry

Visual Faith Ministry is the collaborative effort of on-line and "in-real-life" learning communities to enrich, encourage and enable the vital connections between visual and kinesthetic learning styles and the storytelling of God's faithfulness in our lives.

Visual Faith is reading, reflecting, and responding to God's Word. It welcomes writing, drawing, designs, and color to create reminders of faith that help tell the story for followers of Jesus. Visual Faith reminds us that we are made in the image of a creative God.

Visual Faith honors God's creative sanctification of believers on a daily basis and is the basic process of bringing together our great gifts of prayer and God's Word. It adds visual, kinesthetic, and tactile adaptations that make meaning for us in our daily lives. Visual Faith is a "selfie" of our time with God, helping us to remember, retain, and be ready to share it with others.

In all of these ways and more, Visual Faith helps to answer the question, "What does this mean for me?"

Find more Visual Faith resources at
https://www.visualfaithmin.org/

About Valerie Matyas

Valerie Matyas is a Visual Faith Coach and the Educational Development Consultant for Visual Faith Ministry.

Valerie is a sought-after speaker for retreats, conferences, and workshops. She enjoys presenting visual faith practices to professional church workers and lay people of all ages.

Valerie served as the Lead Illustrator for the hymn journal *When from Death I'm Free* as well as providing illustrations for the following:

What Wondrous Love is This;
Ride On, Ride On in Majesty;
We are All Thieves on a Cross;
Stricken, Smitten, and Afflicted

Valerie lives in Michigan with her clerical wearing husband and four young children.

Meet the Visual Faith Illustrators

Ann Gillaspie
Go to Dark Gethsemane;
I Know that My Redeemer Lives

Ann Gillaspie is a Visual Faith Coach and regular contributor to the Visual Church Year Project. She specializes in hand lettering and enjoys bringing her love for art and faith together as a means to worship God. Ann is a pastor's wife, mom of two grown sons and daughters-in-law, and grandma to two little boys and a little girl.

Katie Helmreich
The King is Calling;
O the Dignity of the Cross

Katie Helmreich is an artist and illustrator, and regularly contributes to the Visual Church Year Project and other Visual Faith resources. She enjoys teaching Visual Faith art classes regularly helping others grow and share in the joy of this experience. Katie lives in Michigan with her engineer/firefighter husband and three kids.

Karen Hunter

This Dust;
We Will Rise

Karen Hunter is a visual faith artist and regular contributor to the Visual Church Year Project and multiple online Visual Faith forums. She loves spending time in the Word and incorporating a variety of visual faith art into her Bible, journals and faith planner. Karen is a wife, mom, former classroom teacher, and Bible Study leader in her home church in Virginia.

Pat Maier

On That Morning;
When I Survey the Wondrous Cross

Pat Maier is a visual faith artist and co-founder of Visual Faith Ministry. She teaches and creates resources for visual processing and was one of the illustrators for The Enduring Word Bible. Pat, a retired educator, lives in Michigan where she is most importantly a wife, mother, and grandmother.

About Kip Fox

Kip and his wife Michelle reside in Scottsdale, Arizona with their son Beau and overly active dog, Jack.

As a nationally recognized songwriter and worship leader, Kip has traveled the country extensively, teaching his songs and leading worship for congregations and gatherings of every shape and size.

His greatest joy is to write and teach new songs that encourage people to see the grace of God in new ways.

He currently serves as Director of Music and Worship at St. Luke Lutheran Church in Mesa, AZ. He also oversees the Center for Worship Leadership's Songwriter Initiative at Concordia University in Irvine, California.

To find out more about his ministry,
or to contact Kip directly,
visit kipfox.com.

Full of love and grace and truth   the King, __ the King is call-ing you.

About Justin Rossow

Rev. Dr. Justin Rossow preaches, teaches, presents, and writes at the intersection of Scripture, culture, and metaphor theory.

With 20 years of ministry experience focused especially on discipleship, Justin brings a refreshing and encouraging voice to the adventure of helping people delight in taking a next step.

Justin is known for his insight and energy, and writes like he talks: with humor, humility, and profound dependence on Jesus.

Justin and his wife Miriam live in Michigan with their four children.

He is the founder of Next Step Press and The Next Step Community.

You can follow him online at
justinrossow.com
or on YouTube, Facebook,
Twitter, or Patreon.

About Next Step Press

You're trying to follow Jesus; that's awesome!

We want to help.

Next Step Press is a ministry devoted to producing engaging resources that help you delight in taking a next step following Jesus.

When you need to find your path forward, either as an individual or in a small group, we're there for you. One size does not fit all when it comes to discipleship; find something that works for you.

When the task of leading a group feels overwhelming, we can help with that, too. Everything we design for congregations and leaders will support your effort to build and sustain a culture of discipleship, no matter the size of your community. From books, to sermon series, to staff training, to weekend retreats, we've got your back.

We know it's not easy to follow Jesus, and the Next Step Press team wants to alleviate the burden of being a Christian with the joy of being a follower.

What's your next step?

Find out more at
www.FindMyNextStep.org

The Next Step Community

The Next Step Community is a group of people, like you, who need other people to help them take a next step following Jesus.

You won't find any preconceived notions or quick fixes here; just real people trying to follow Jesus in real life. You are welcome to join in!

We follow Jesus better when we follow Him together, so we invite you to share what you experienced in this Hymn Journal by emailing Curator@FindMyNextStep.org.

What experiments helped and why?

Did you customize anything or try a variation that seemed to work for you?

What did you share with someone else, and how did it go?

When you share your story of taking a next step, you help someone else take theirs.

Come, join the community at
community.FindMyNextStep.org

SDG

Made in the USA
Monee, IL
01 March 2020